I Can Do It

Written by Sally Featherstone and Clare Beswick

Illustrated by Martha Hardy

A Little Baby Book

Published by Featherstone Education

About Little Baby Books

'Birth to Three Matters' (DfES Sure Start 2002) the framework for effective practice with babies and very young children, sends a clear unequivocal message underlining the importance of home and family working together with practitioners to lay the best possible foundations for life and learning. It is a recognition and celebration of the individuality of babies and young children. It provides a wealth of guidance and support to those with responsibility for their care and education.

The Little Baby Book series build on the principles of the guidance and provide a practical handbook, with a wealth of easy to follow ideas and activities for babies and young children from birth to three.

The Birth to three framework identifies four aspects which highlight the skills and competence of babies and young children as well as showing the link between growth, learning, development and the environment in which they are cared for and educated.

These four aspects of the Framework are:
* A strong child (Purple Books)   * A skilful communicator (Pink Books)
* A competent learner (Green Books)   * A healthy child (Blue Books)

All the activities use objects and resources readily available in homes and settings. They allow babies and children to develop at their own pace, to make unhurried discoveries and allow for much repetition as well as trying out of new ideas. It encourages children to become increasingly independent, making their own choices. All the activities require the careful and skilful support of an adult. The role of the adult is included in the step-by-step 'What you do section.

About 'I Can Do It'

I Can Do It is part of the Little Baby Books series and focuses on the aspect –
A Strong Child.

Within this aspect there are four components:
* Me Myself and I
* Being Acknowledged and Affirmed
* Developing Self-assurance
* A Sense of Belonging

Developing self-assurance, the focus of this Little Baby Book, is about babies and young children becoming able to trust and rely on their own abilities. In order to do this, children need a sense of themselves as a separate being, with strengths and skills, and growing into a sense of self worth and competence. The activities in this book aim to enable babies and young children to:

* learn about themselves
* reach out to others
* recognise what they can do
* experience success
* gain confidence
* work with others
* take responsibility
* use their imagination and ingenuity

* become independent
* think about their achievements
* feel successful
* know and appreciate their abilities
* recognise skills in others
* enjoy responsibility and success
* know that adults and other children
   value them and their contribution

Your role as practitioner or parent will be varied and will include:
* Facilitating   * Observing   * Prompting   * Negotiating
* Supporting   * Imitating   * Celebrating   * Acknowledging

Confidence and
competence

Aspect:
A Strong Child
Components:
developing self
assurance

3

Why is developing self-assurance so important for babies and young children?

Being confident and self assured are fundamental to successful growth and learning. Children need to grow up secure, strong and confident of their own abilities..

Babies and young children do not develop self assurance on their own. They need sensitive 'switched on' carers and practitioners who prioritise children's needs, celebrate their learning and share their natural curiosity about the world. Practitioners need to be skilful observers, sensitively attuned to each individual baby or child. They need to be focused and purposeful, unhurried and planned in their support and genuinely intrigued by the child's voyage of discovery and personal growth.

'I Can Do It' focuses on the range of discoveries and ideas that underpin young children's development of confidence and competence. The activities in this book support practitioners in providing rich and varied opportunities for babies and very young children to become both confident and competent learners. These include:

Reaching out to others	Having their achievements celebrated
Touching and feeling	Learning new games, skills and actions
Using hands, fingers and thumbs	Overcoming difficulties and fears
Holding and manipulating objects	Instigating and copying movements
Feeling successful in movement	Following, copying, leading
Exploring independently	Thinking and reflecting on what they can do.

All the activities use objects and resources readily available in homes and nursery settings. They allow babies and children to develop at their own pace and to make unhurried discoveries. They allow for much repetition as well as trying out of new ideas.

Watch, listen, reflect

Assessing babies' and children's learning is a difficult process, but we do know that any assessment must be based on careful observation of children in action.

On each activity page, you will see a box labelled **Watch, listen, reflect.** This box contains suggestions of what you might look and listen for as you work and play with the babies and children. Much of the time you will watch, listen and <u>remember</u>, using your knowledge of early years and of the children and reflecting on the progress of the individual child. These informal observations will help you to plan the next day's or week's activities.

However, sometimes, what you see is new evidence - something you have never seen the child do before, or something which concerns you. In these cases you might make a written note of the achievements you see, and the date and time you observed it. You will use these notes for a range different purposes, and some of these are:

- 👁 to remind you of the event or achievement (it's easy to forget in a busy setting!)
- 👁 to use in discussion with your manager or other practitioners
- 👁 to contribute to the child's profile or record
- 👁 to discuss with parents
- 👁 to help with identifying or supporting additional needs
- 👁 to help with planning for individuals
- 👁 to make sure you tell everyone about the child's achievements.

Observation is a crucial part of the complex job you do, and time spent observing and listening to children is never wasted.

Confidence and competence

Aspect:
A Strong Child
Components:
developing self assurance

5

I Can Do It

Confidence and competence

Keeping safe

Safety must be the top priority when working with any baby or young child, at nursery or at home. All the activities in Little Baby Books are suitable for under threes. You will already have a health and safety policy but here are just a few top tips for safe playing with babies and young children.

Watch for choking hazards.

Young babies and children naturally explore toys by bringing them to their mouths. This is fine, but always check that toys are clean. If you are concerned, buy a choke measure from a high street baby shop.

Never leave babies or young children unattended.

They are naturally inquisitive and this needs to be encouraged, BUT they need you watch out for them. Make sure you are always there.

Check for sharp edges.

Some everyday objects or wooden toys can splinter. Check all toys and equipment regularly. Don't leave this to chance – make a rota.

Ribbons and string.

Mobiles and toys tied to baby gyms are a great to encourage looking and reaching, but do check regularly that they are fastened securely. Ribbons and string are fascinating for babies and children of all ages – but they can be a choking hazard.

Clean spaces.

Babies are natural explorers. They need clean floors. Store outdoor shoes away from the under threes area.

Sitters and standers.

Make sure of a soft landing for babies and young children just getting there with sitting and standing balance. Put a pillow behind babies who are just starting to sit. Keep the area clear of hard objects, such as wooden bricks. Look out for trip hazards for crawlers and walkers.

High and low chairs.

Make sure babies and young children are fastened securely into high chairs and that chairs are moved out of the way when not in use. Use a low chair and table for young children. Try to make a foot-rest if their feet don't reach the ground. Watch out for chairs that tip easily.

6

Contents

I Can Do It

Confidence and competence

Aspect:
A Strong Child
Components:
developing self assurance

Confidence and
competence

**Heads up lookers
and communicators**

Aspect:
A Strong Child
Components:
developing self
assurance

Reach out -
reaching and touching

What you need

* a blanket or cushion

What you do

1. Hold the baby securely so they can see your face.
2. make sure you have the baby's attention.
3. Open your mouth wide and encourage the baby to reach out and touch your face. Praise any movement towards you with their hands or arms.
4. Now put the baby on the blanket or cushion on the floor.
5. Lean over the baby until your face is within reach. Talk to them and encourage them to reach up and touch your face. Remember to give praise and smiles for every effort at reaching, touching, holding.

another idea:
* hang a small object round your neck and lean over so the baby can reach up for it.

Ready for more?

🖐 Put a light scarf over your head and let the baby pull it off.
🖐 Stand in front of a mirror and let the baby reach out for the reflection.
🖐 Walk round your setting and feel different textures.

Individual needs

☼ Some babies will need you to take their hand(s) gently to your face or an object.
☼ Put a shiny ribbon in your hair or hang a shiny object round your neck.
☼ Allow plenty of time for babies and children with poor head control to lift their heads to look and focus on you.

Tiny Tip

✳ babies will respond to sounds - use a sound to attract their attention.

Watch, listen, reflect

👁 Watch how the baby reacts to being near your face. Look at their expressions, follow their gaze and listen for sounds
👁 Watch for favourite sounds or expressions which attract or amuse them.
👁 Watch how they touch, pat and stroke your face or objects.

Working together

Parents could:

* Spend a few minutes every day holding their babies and encouraging them to reach out and touch .
* Remember to give their babies plenty of praise and smiles.

Practitioners could:

* Take some photos of the babies while they are reaching and touching.
* Make a list of all the different ways babies explore objects and look out for these with their key worker children.

I Can Do It

Confidence and competence

What are they learning?

are they
  looking?
  exploring?
  holding?
  grasping?
  making sounds?
this leads to
  * reaching
  * turn taking
  * sense of self

9

I Can Do It

Confidence and competence

Heads up lookers and communicators

Aspect:
A Strong Child
Components:
developing self assurance

Take this -
taking hold

What you need

* a few everyday objects, each small and light enough for the baby to hold and release eg a small whisk, a little wooden spoon or baby spoon, a plastic lid, a little plastic bottle

What you do

1. Clear a space to remove other distractions and make sure the baby is sitting well supported.
2. Sit opposite the baby and hold out one of the objects. Talk to the baby and encourage them to take the object. Hold it close enough for them to take it in their hand, but far enough away so they have to reach out.
3. Let them play with the object, talking to them about it as they do, and giving smiles and praise for holding.
4. Offer them another object (they will probably drop the first one!) and give them praise for taking it.
5. Allow them time with the objects to just play and experiment.

another idea:
* Try some crinkly paper or textured fabric.

Ready for more?

🖐 Make a treasure basket for the babies to play with. Fill it with interesting objects to explore and hold.
🖐 Make a Pat mat from a small zip lock bag filled with cotton wool, crinkly paper or paint!

Individual needs

☼ Make sure the objects are light enough for the child to grip and wave about.

☼ Attach bells or small lengths of ribbon to attract attention.

☼ Give them plenty of time to explore the objects. Sit with them as they do so, giving encouragement and praise for effort.

Tiny Tip

✱ You can get baskets from florists, garden centres and charity shops.

Watch, listen, reflect

👁 Watch for grasping as well as reaching.

👁 Observe which objects are most appealing to the baby

👁 Change the objects frequently and watch how they respond to new ones.

👁 Listen for vocalisation and sounds.

Working together

Parents could:

* Create their own treasure basket of simple objects at home.
* Give their baby some real things to play with as well as bought toys.

Practitioners could:

* Suggest items for the parents to use in a treasure basket for their baby to explore at home.
* Take some photos of babies playing with everyday objects, so parents understand that play doesn't have to cost money!

I Can Do It

Confidence and competence

What are they learning?

are they
　looking?
　reaching?
　holding?
　grasping?
　making sounds?
this leads to
　* taking hold
　* selecting
　* sense of self

11

Confidence and competence

Heads up lookers and communicators

Aspect:
A Strong Child
Components:
developing self assurance

Shake it! - shaking and rattling

What you need

* some things that rattle - tins with beads or pasta in, baby rattles, bells, boxes, purses with coins, snack tubes with pebbles, zip lock bags with beads

What you do

1. Collect together a few rattling objects. Make sure they are light enough for the baby to hold and shake.
2. Sit opposite the baby and pick up one of the rattlers. Shake it to attract their attention.
3. Say 'Look. Shake, shake, shake'.
4. Offer them the rattle and wait for them to respond to it. Give it a little shake to tempt them.
5. Try again with another rattler.
6. Allow plenty of time for listening and for the baby to respond. Give plenty of smiles and praise for their efforts.

another idea:
* Try having a rattle each and sharing the shaking.

Ready for more?

- Try rattling under a blanket or cloth and see if the baby can pull the blanket off to get the rattle.
- Try the games with some simple shakers and other simple musical instruments.

Individual needs

- Give them plenty of time to focus on the rattle and reach out for it.
- Remember to give praise with your expression as well as your voice.
- Allow plenty of time for babies and children with poor head control to lift their heads to look and focus.

Tiny Tip

❋ Use glass beads in clear plastic bottles, or coloured water in a leak proof container.

Watch, listen, reflect

- Look at facial expressions, follow their gaze and listen for sounds.
- Observe which rattles are most appealing to the baby.
- Look at the different ways they explore the rattles - banging, shaking, waving. Watch for expressions of pleasure and smiles at your smiles.

Working together

Parents could:

* Make some simple shakers at home, using everyday containers and objects.
* Spend time playing 'Shake, shake, shake' with their baby, and praising their efforts .

Practitioners could:

* Make a display of simple shakers made from everyday objects, to give parents ideas.
* Hang rattles over changing tables and mats.

I Can Do It

Confidence and competence

What are they learning?

are they
grasping?
shaking?
smiling?
listening?
this leads to
* a sense of success
* a sense of self

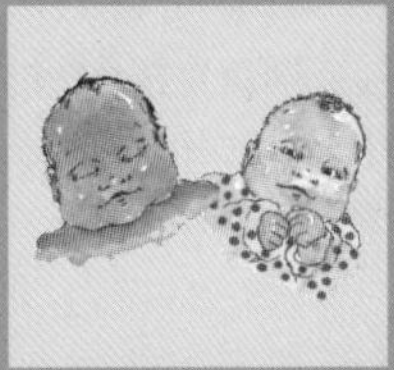

Sitters, standers and explorers

Aspect:
A Strong Child
Components:
developing self assurance

Pass it back -
to and fro passing

What you need
* a treasure basket or collection of small familiar objects

What you do

1. Sit opposite the baby on the floor. Choose an object from the basket.
2. Offer it to the baby and encourage them to take hold of it.
3. Hold your hand out for the object and say 'Give the ..... to me.' Encourage them by touching the object to attract their attention. Wait to see if they give the object to you. Praise them if they do - smile and say 'Good boy/girl, you gave me the .... Thank you.'
4. If the don't give you the object, touch it gently again and see if they release it. Use your judgement to decide whether to gently take the object back and play the game again, or to try again another time.

another idea:
* Try holding out tin or box for them to put the object in.

Ready for more?

- Play passing games at change time, or snack time.
- Play games when you ask them to pass objects to other children. Praise them for doing this - it's difficult!

Individual needs

☼ Put objects in front of the baby and let them pass them to you as a first stage in this game.

☼ Try passing plates and cups for drinks etc. Then ask them to pass them back when they have finished.

Tiny Tip

✳ Try charity shops for treasure basket objects. Make sure they are clean before use!

Watch, listen, reflect

👁 Watch to see when children offer objects to other children or adults. This is the cue you need for starting the passing to and fro game.

👁 Does the baby understand the outstretched hand 'give me' gesture?

👁 Watch for expressions of pleasure and achievement.

Working together

Parents could:

* Play passing games at home with their children at bath time, meal time.
* Play My hand, your hand, piling up hands one on top of each other.

Practitioners could:

* Make opportunities for babies and children to pass things to you during nappy changing, snack and other times.
* Show children by expression and words that giving things to others is an achievement.

I Can Do It

Confidence and competence

What are they learning?

are they
  passing?
  offering?
  releasing objects?
  using fingers?
this leads to
  * a sense of self and others
  * simple games and turn taking

Sitters, standers and explorers

Aspect:
A Strong Child
Components:
developing self assurance

Hands together - clapping and patting

What you need

* no special equipment

What you do

1. Sit opposite the baby on the floor or sit together in a chair so you are facing each other.
2. Hold your hands out and see if the baby offers their hands. If not, gently take their hands and clap them together, saying 'Clapping, clapping, we are clapping'.
3. If the baby is enjoying it, try singing 'Pat a cake, Pat a cake, baker's man' while you gently hold their hands.
4. Hold your hands out and let the baby pat their hands on yours, or get very close and let them pat their hands on your face. Praise their efforts at patting and clapping.

another idea:
* Try a tin lid or plastic mirror for patting games.

Ready for more?

- Have patting fun in paint, tomato sauce or shaving foam.
- Make some pat mats with different textures for the baby to pat and grasp.

Individual needs

☼ Give young children plenty of opportunities for patting and clapping in simple games. hold their hands if they want or need it.

☼ Some babies and young children may need help getting their hands to connect with each other.

Tiny Tip

❋ Try a tambourine for some noisy patting fun!

Watch, listen, reflect

👁 Watch for control in bringing their hands together in front of them - this is a key developmental stage.

👁 Note whether they copy you as you clap and sing.

👁 Listen for any sounds, words and other joining in with songs rhymes and actions.

Working together

Parents could:

* Sing simple, made up action songs with their babies and children.
* Play a patting and clapping game with their child as they travel to and from nursery.

Practitioners could:

* Make a simple leaflet of traditional clapping songs and movement rhymes for parents to take home.
* Ask parents about their children's favourite songs and rhymes, and include these in their work.

I Can Do It

Confidence and competence

What are they learning?

are they
  using two hands?
  watching and copying?
  sharing fun?
  clapping?
this leads to
  * hand control
  * enjoying simple games

17

Sitters, standers and explorers

Aspect:
A Strong Child
Components:
developing self assurance

Get it! -
following and fetching

What you need

* a wind-up toy, a small toy with wheels, a small soft ball.

What you do

This game is suitable for babies who are just beginning to crawl or are already on the move.

1. Sit with the baby on the floor, indoors or outside.
2. Show the baby the toys you have selected and look at them together.
3. Now roll the toy away from the baby and say 'Get it!' Use the baby's name as you point to the moving toy. As they move towards the toy, encourage them with words and gestures.
4. When the baby has reached the toy, say 'Good try! Can you bring it back?'. Praise them when they bring the toy back to play the game again, but don't worry if they don't! Just go and join them where they are.

another idea: Try the game with bubbles or clean feathers.

Ready for more?

👋 Play the game with a toy on a string, pulling it behind you so the baby can crawl and catch. Keep close, don't go too fast and stop when they are tired!

Individual needs

☼ Don't roll the toy too far away.

☼ Remember that some babies and young children may need you to demonstrate how to play. If they find it difficult, try first with a toy on a string that they can follow.

☼ Babies in buggies may need two adults - one to run, the other to chase with the buggy!

Tiny Tip

✴ Try charity shops for toys on strings, or other objects that roll or run on wheels.

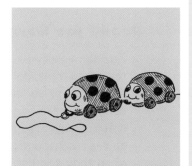

Watch, listen, reflect

👁 Look at the baby's response - do they understand how to play this simple game?

👁 Do they respond to your praise and smiles? Do they show a sense of achievement and fun?

👁 Note developments in grasping and carrying objects, and look at how they move along the floor. Every child is different!

Working together

Parents could:

* Play these chasing games at home or in the garden, to help develop crawling skills.

* Remember to praise their children regularly - building their sense of self esteem and achievement.

Practitioners could:

* Talk about all the gentle games you can play to help babies get on the move.

* Explain the benefit of adult involvement in games, so children get feedback on their achievements.

I Can Do It

Confidence and competence

What are they learning?

are they
   on the move?
   enjoying a game?
   fetching toys?
   seeing you smile?
   reaching?
this leads to
   * motor control
   * recognising achievement and success

I Can Do It

Confidence and competence

Sitters, standers and explorers

Aspect:
A Strong Child
Components:
developing self assurance

Put it in, get it out -
heuristic play with tins

What you need

* some tins or containers (use sterilised food cans with any sharp edges smoothed out)
* lengths of chain, shells, corks, bottle caps, pebbles

What you do

This activity can involve two or three babies, but they each need their own set of tins and objects.

1. Sit with babies during the whole of this activity. Make sure they are well balanced and can reach the objects.
2. Give them plenty of time to explore the tins and things.
3. Most babies will need no instructions! They will immediately begin to fill and empty the tins.
4. If they need help, just show them once, or play alongside them with your own collection of tin and things.
5. Let the babies play for as long as they wish. Some will play for a long time! Keep watching them to ensure safety.

Background information:
Look at 'People Under Three' by Eleanor Goldschmeid for more information about Heuristic Play with objects.

Ready for more?

- Add some dolly pegs (the old fashioned wooden ones) to slip on the edges of the tins.
- Offer a collection of gift boxes to put the objects in.
- Try purses and real or pretend money.

Individual needs

☼ Check the objects to make sure the baby can lift them easily to put them in a tin.

☼ Be vigilant when children are playing with objects that could be swallowed or chewed. They may need longer to explore objects and find out which ones are edible!

Safety Tip

✳ Make sure the tins are clean and safe, and the objects are not too small.

Watch, listen, reflect

This is a very good activity for a longer, more complex observation.

👁 Note how well they concentrate on this activity.

👁 Look at the development of fine motor movements, fingers and thumbs, pincer grip, hand eye co-ordination, use of both hands.

👁 Give eye contact, smiles and encouragement as they work.

Working together

Parents could:

* Make a treasure basket for their child to play with at home.
* Watch their child playing and tell practitioners what they see.

Practitioners could:

* Put up a list of the possible contents of a treasure basket.
* Make some treasure baskets for the children to play with in the setting.

See the end of this book for ideas and books about Treasure Baskets.

I Can Do It

Confidence and competence

What are they learning?

are they
    using two hands?
    sitting steadily?
    concentrating?
    using fingers?
    exploring?
this leads to
    * fine motor control
    * ability to play alone

**Movers, shakers
and players**

Aspect:
A Strong Child
Components:
developing self
assurance

22

Put it in, put it on -
posting and stacking

What you need

* make a simple posting toy from a small box. Just make one hole on the top of the box and use bricks, cotton reels, coins, socks, Duplo bricks or other objects to post.

What you do

You can play this game with one or two children. Even a simple, one-hole box gives young children a real sense of success.

1. Sit opposite the children with the posting toy between you and all the posting shapes on the floor.
2. Show the children how to post the objects in the hole.
3. Now offer one of the babies an object and encourage them to post it in the hole. Give them plenty of praise for efforts and success.
4. Take turns to post objects in the box until they are all gone. Say 'All gone!' and 'More?'
5. If they want to play again, tip the objects out and start again.

another idea:

* Make additional holes in the box, or make a smaller hole.

Ready for more?

- Play a game with a stacking toy, taking turns to put a ring on or to balance a beaker.
- Try a simple Feely Bag or box, and play taking things out of the bag and putting them back in again.

Individual needs

☼ Make a small box with a big posting hole. Cover it with shiny paper to attract the child's attention.

☼ Put a metal tin lid in the bottom of the box so the objects make a noise as you take turns to post them in.

Tiny Tip

✽ Collect boxes of all shapes and sizes for making into posting toys, and hair scrunchies to thread on a post for a bargain toy.

Watch, listen, reflect

👁 Look for emerging concepts of taking turns.

👁 Watch how they use their hands and fingers to grasp and release the objects into the boxes.

👁 Listen for words such as 'All gone'.

👁 Watch for signs of enjoyment and achievement, and developing concentration.

Working together

Parents could:

* Make a simple posting box at home from a cereal packet or small box.
* Practice turn taking by passing toys to each other, and passing a spoon between them at mealtime.

Practitioners could:

* Put some posting and threading toys in the Toy Library.
* Watch individual children for emerging schemas of posting, wrapping, filling and emptying. Share observations with parents.

What are they learning?

are they
taking turns?
holding and releasing?
enjoying success?
this leads to
* co-operating
* self esteem
* playing games

I Can Do It

Confidence and competence

Movers, shakers and players

Aspect:
A Strong Child
Components:
developing self assurance

24

In you go! -
tunnels and tents

What you need

* a play tunnel or a drape over some chairs to make a tunnel
* a pop up tent or home made fabric tent

What you do

This game is very popular for groups of two children, and gives them a real sense of achievement.

1. Let the children watch and help you put up the tunnel and/or tent. Talk to them about what you are doing.
2. Sit near the entrance to the tunnel and encourage the children to take turns going through the tunnel.
3. If they are cautious or anxious, put a soft toy at the end of the tunnel, or make it shorter.
4. Praise the children as they emerge from the other end of the tunnel. Remember that for some children, this is a real test of bravery and endurance!

another idea:
* Go through the tunnel yourself and get them to clap you for your bravery!

Ready for more?

🖐 Make the tunnel longer or put the pop up tent at the end for them to crawl into.

🖐 Make a junior obstacle race outside with tunnels, small steps, tents and other things to climb.

Individual needs

☼ Children with restricted movement will love going through a tunnel with you!.

☼ Hang some ribbons or bells from a sheet of fabric and hold it over their head to make a roof.

☼ Use net or transparent fabric for anxious children, so they can see out.

Tiny Tip

✻ Try seaside shops for cheap tents and tunnels. Or use a parachute or big piece of fabric.

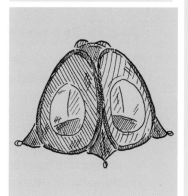

Watch, listen, reflect

👁 Watch the way children explore the tunnels and tents.

👁 Look at levels of confidence and fear. Note particular difficulties, such as going in, or bends in tunnels.

👁 Listen and watch for expressions and sounds of success. Be vigilant for children who are frightened of being enclosed.

Working together

Parents could:

* help their children make dens and tents at home.
* Have fun under the bed-clothes when they get up, or when they make the beds.

Practitioners could:

* Put photos of simple home made tents and dens on the parents' notice board.
* Talk with parents about fears and excitement in their own children, and the importance of help-ing children to overcome their fears.

I Can Do It

Confidence and competence

What are they learning?

are they
taking safe risks?
enjoying it?
experiencing success?
playing together?
this leads to
* co-operating
* self esteem
* overcoming fears

Confidence and
competence

**Movers, shakers
and players**

Aspect:
A Strong Child
Components:
developing self
assurance

26

Up and down -
stairs, steps, slides

What you need

* a small set of children's steps
  (as in picture) OR
* some safe steps or stairs
  indoors or outside

What you do

Climbing up and down steps and stairs needs plenty of
practice and praise. Play this game with one or two children.
1. Start at the bottom of the steps.
2. Hold the children's hands and climb the steps with them.
   Say or sing *'Up we go, up we go, one two, up we go'*.
3. When you get to the top, say *'Well done, we climbed up.
   What can we see from up at the top?'*
4. Turn round and step down the steps, singing *'Down we go,
   down we go, one two, down we go'*.
4. Go slowly, so the children have time to put both feet on
   each step if they need to.
5. Repeat this song and movement several times.
another idea:
* Practice singing and walking up the steps of a low slide.

Ready for more?

☝ Put heavy bricks or
blocks (or two sets of
play steps) together to
make an 'up and down'
staircase.
✋ Make some little steps
with bricks for teddies
and dolls to go up and
down.

Individual needs

☼ Make sure there are rails beside steps in your setting and garden.

☼ Give children plenty of time and praise for this difficult skill..

☼ Remember, going up is much easier than going down!

Safety Tip!

❄ Babies and young children should never be left unattended near stairs until they can manage going up AND down safely.

Watch, listen, reflect

👁 Note how soon children can climb steps on their own. Look at how they climb - one foot, both feet, one foot, both feet, or one foot at a time up the steps.

👁 Remember that children learn better if they have plenty of praise. Observe yourself and other practitioners to make sure you give plenty of feedback.

Working together

Parents could:

★ Give their child plenty of opportunity to climb steps with help and independently.

★ Let children walk along low walls and steps when they are out on walks.

Practitioners could:

★ Make sure steps and stairs are safely used, and protected with stair gates when adults are not around.

★ Help parents to understand safe ways of learning about steps and stairs.

I Can Do It

Confidence and competence

What are they learning?

are they
    climbing?
    practicing?
    experiencing
    success?
    being praised?
this leads to
    * self esteem
    * confidence
    * self assurance

27

Movers, shakers and players

Aspect:
A Strong Child
Components:
developing self assurance

Snip, snap! - cutting and snipping

What you need

* safe scissors
* plenty of paper - eg magazine pages, recycled paper, junk mail, wallpaper, wrapping paper, envelopes

What you do

This activity is about confidence and self assurance in cutting - not 'cutting out'. A small group would enjoy it.

1. Cut some of the paper into long thin strips, so that the children can snip across them in one cut.
2. Leave some of the paper in bigger pieces..
3. Sit at a table with the children, and talk about cutting and snipping as they work. Give plenty of encouragement.
4. Help children if they need it, by holding the paper as they snip, or by putting your hand over theirs on the scissors.
5. Help them to snip the long pieces into bits, or snip round the edges of bigger pieces.

another idea:
* Snip the edges of pieces of coloured paper and use them as place mats for snack time.

Ready for more?

- Sometimes, let them fringe the edges of their drawings or paintings.
- Snip lengths of coloured or shiny paper and stick them on a strip of card for an individual crown.

Individual needs

✿ Search out some specialised scissors for children with poor grip, and for left handers.

✿ Sit facing the child and hold the paper so they can snip from their side.

✿ Sometimes let the child hold the paper as you snip.

Tiny Tip

✳ Scissors must be sharp enough to cut, or the children will get frustrated and discouraged.

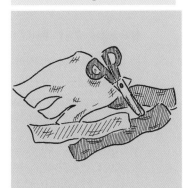

Watch, listen, reflect

👁 Watch the way children hold the scissors and give plenty of encouragement and modelling to help them improve.

👁 Listen to them talk as they cut - you will get some interesting observations!

👁 Note how well they concentrate on learning and practising this difficult skill.

Working together

Parents could:

* Let their children practice with suitable scissors at home.
* be patient when children just snip and snip!

Practitioners could:

* Advise parents about suitable scissors for their children.
* make sure children have plenty of safe practice with snipping at the early stage of learning scissor skills.

I Can Do It

Confidence and competence

What are they learning?

are they
    concentrating?
    experiencing
    success?
    using both hands?
This leads to
    * self assurance
    * fine motor
    skills
    * confidence

Confidence and competence

Movers, shakers and players

Aspect:
A Strong Child
Components:
developing self assurance

Peg it! -
pegboard play

What you need

* wooden or plastic peg boards with holes
* different coloured pegs in small bowls

What you do

This activity supports fine motor control and a sense of achievement. Three or four children could play together.

1. Sit with the children at a table.
2. Talk about the pegs and peg boards and model how they are used.
3. Play alongside the children, making patterns, putting the pegs in and taking them out. Talk about what you are doing as you work.
4. Look at the children's work too, giving praise and encouragement. looking at each other's patterns, talking about colours and shapes.

another idea:

* Try making a one-line pattern for them to copy. Then get them to make one for you to copy.

Ready for more?

- Roll out a big piece of dough and use it as a group peg board. When it is full of holes, roll it out again.
- Take turns with one or two children to put a peg in a board. You could have a colour each.

Individual needs

☼ Make sure the pegs are easy to put in and get out.

☼ Look for big pegs and boards with bigger holes.

☼ Stick the board down to the table with blutack to steady it for children with poor motor control.

Tiny Tip

✳ Float the pegs in a bowl of bubbly water to make a different sort of game!

Watch, listen, reflect

👁 Watch to see if the children can follow the simple routine and rules of this game.

👁 Listen to how the children negotiate with each other. Listen for short phrases where they predict what might happen next.

👁 Look to see if the children have the confidence to join in with this familiar song.

Working together

Parents could:

* Chop up some straws into short lengths and make a game of pushing them into flour and water pastry or wet sand.
* Try clipping clothes pegs onto a low level washing line..

Practitioners could:

* Put some pegs and boards in the toy library or loan collection.
* Provide some 'take home' dough or a recipe for it.

I Can Do It

Confidence and competence

What are they learning?

are they
  concentrating?
  using fingers and hands?
  having fun?
  making patterns?
this leads to
  * concentration
  * self assurance
  * fine motor skills

31

Confidence and competence

Walkers, talkers and pretenders

Aspect:
A Strong Child
Components:
developing self assurance

Catch it, kick it -
ball play

What you need
* a soft ball, big enough to catch, but not too big!

What you do
Play this game in a big space, indoors or outside, with a small group. Throw and catch, kicking and rolling are all good confidence boosters as well as practice for fine and whole body control.

1. Begin by playing informally and responsively with the children, throwing, catching, rolling, kicking. Use each child's name, and give them plenty of praise and feedback on their actions.
2. Encourage them to call each other's names as they pass or kick the ball.

another idea:
* If the children find the ball difficult to handle, try a bean bag, or a pair of rolled socks.

Ready for more?
🖐 Take turns throwing balls, bean bags or rolled socks into a bucket.
🖐 Try throwing wet sponge balls at a wall or fence.
🖐 Have a child sized football goal outside.

Individual needs

☼ Use a 'Koosh' ball with children who have hand control difficulties.
☼ Try rolling a beach ball to children with mobility problems.
☼ Use bright coloured balls and bean bags for children with visual problems.

Tiny Tip

❊ Look in catalogues and stores for different sorts of balls. let children choose which ones to use.

Watch, listen, reflect

👁 Watch how the children use their hands, arms and feet. Look for dominant hands and feet.
👁 Note the children who can catch with both hands.
👁 Watch for aiming, releasing, calling other children's attention etc.
👁 Listen for words and sentences to describe their own movements.

Working together

Parents could:

★ Play throw, catch and kick games with their children.
★ Practice aiming and releasing - perhaps by throwing dirty clothes into the laundry basket.

Practitioners could:

* Give children plenty of opportunities to play throw, catch and kick outside.
* Talk to parents about what they observe and see if the children show the same behaviours at home.

I Can Do It

Confidence and competence

What are they learning?

are they
    having fun?
    anticipating?
    using hands and
    feet?
    gaining confi-
    dence?
this leads to
    * confidence
    * a sense of
    achievement

Confidence and
competence

**Walkers, talkers
and pretenders**

Aspect:
A Strong Child
Components:
developing self
assurance

I play, you play -
a sound copying game

What you need
* some simple musical instruments or sound makers such as
  bells, shakers, rattles, drums,
  tambourines or sticks, boxes,
  tins, trays, saucepans, shakers
  etc if you haven't got instruments.

What you do
This activity is suitable for a small group of children. You
    need enough sound makers for one for each child and one
    for you. You can all have the same instrument or a mixture.
1. Sit in a circle with the children, indoors or outside.
2. Offer them an instrument each, and let them experiment
   and explore the sounds it can make. Give plenty of praise
   and feedback as they shake, rattle and bang.
3. When they have had a good go at making sounds, ask them
   to listen and copy as you make a sound. Make a simple
   sound, pause for them to copy, praise their efforts, then
   make another sound or short pattern.

another idea:
* Ask the children to make sounds and patterns for you to
  copy. Give plenty of praise for listening and responding.

Ready for more?

* Make up a simple copy-
  ing song, such as 'Copy
  me, copy me, Listen
  first, then copy me.'
* Play clapping games,
  making simple clapping
  patterns for children
  to copy.

Individual needs

☼ If children have difficulty using both hands, fix an instrument to the table or a chair, or hold it for them to play.

☼ Give plenty of time for exploring sound makers and what they can do. Don't move on to the copying game too quickly. Some children will find it easier if you copy their sounds.

Tiny Tip

✳ Clapping and playing instruments helps children to develop their brains as well as their bodies.

Watch, listen, reflect

👁 Note how individuals concentrate and listen. Are they developing the ability to listen and copy what they hear?

👁 Can they wait for a turn and listen to each other?

👁 Look for signs of enjoyment and a sense of achievement as they play and copy each other.

Working together

Parents could:

* Use familiar household items to make music with their children.
* Sing nursery rhymes and songs every day, perhaps on the way to nursery or pre-school.

Practitioners could:

* Make a booklet of ideas for making musical instruments from found, recycled and everyday materials. Offer this to parents and carers.
* Play clapping games every day in spare minutes or at the change of activities.

I Can Do It

Confidence and competence

What are they learning?

are they
  listening?
  anticipating?
  concentrating?
  enjoying music?
  taking turns?
this leads to
  * belonging
  * enjoying music making
  * simple rules

35

**Walkers, talkers
and pretenders**

Aspect:
A Strong Child
Components:
developing self
assurance

36

Necklaces and strings -
threading with beads

What you need
* wooden or plastic beads of
  various sizes, shapes and
  colours
* threading strings or laces
* bowls or a builder's tray to
  keep the beads in one place!

What you do
This activity is suitable for a small group. You can play at a
   table of on the floor, indoors or outside.
1. Put the beads and strings or laces in containers or on a
   big tray (It's really frustrating for everyone if the beads
   keep escaping!).
2. Sit with the children and show them how to thread the
   beads (make sure there is a knot in the end of the string
   to stop the beads falling off.
3. Make your own string, talking about what you are doing,
   which beads you are choosing, shapes and sizes.
4. Help any child who needs it, and give praise for effort -
   threading is difficult!

another idea:
* Use past a tubes for a different sort of threading game.

Ready for more?
* Just put out two or
  three colours of beads,
  different shapes and
  sizes, to encourage
  pattern making.
* Thread ribbons, string
  or strips of torn fabric
  or paper through
  garden mesh or a
  fence.

Individual needs

- ☼ Children with fine motor difficulties may need a lot of help. Make sure the .
- ☼ Try treading sections of cardboard tube - painted or covered with foil or shiny paper.
- ☼ Hang strings of beads where children can reach and feel them.

Tiny Tip

�֍ Use big beads, so they can't be swallowed or put in ears or nostrils!

Watch, listen, reflect

- 👁 Note how children are using both hands together to thread the beads.
- 👁 Look for the development of concentration and attention.
- 👁 Watch how children respond to praise and encouragement, and how this affects their ability to keep persevering, even when something is difficult to do.

Working together

Parents could:

- ✷ Thread cardboard tubes, pasta tubes or beads at home.
- ✷ Tie and thread strings through garden fences.

Practitioners could:

- ✷ Explain to parents the importance of threading games to later learning in reading and writing.
- ✷ Take some photos of the children doing these activities so parents cans see how hard they are working.

I Can Do It

Confidence and competence

What are they learning?

are they
  using both hands?
  concentrating?
  looking?
  talking?
this leads to
  * fine motor control
  * sustained attention
  * self esteem

**Walkers, talkers
and pretenders**

Aspect:
A Strong Child
Components:
developing self
assurance

Make it work -
using ICT

What you need
* a simple piece of electronic
  equipment - a simple computer
  with an early years programme,
  a programmable toy, children's
  tape recorder, simple CD play-
  er, toy mobile phone

What you do
This activity works best with two children, so they can have
  plenty of access to the equipment.
1. Select a piece of equipment which the children will be
   able to learn to use.
2. Talk about it and explain how to use it. Demonstrate how
   to switch it on, make it work, switch it off.
3. Now let the children take turns to operate the piece of
   equipment. They could also record each other taking or
   singing; take each other's photos, play a computer game.
4. Go slowly, be prepared to repeat the instructions or show
   things again. Give plenty of praise for effort and results.
another idea:
* Get children who know to show younger ones how to work
  things, with you to help and ensure safe play.

Ready for more?
* Show children how to
  select and print their
  own photos. Display
  these with a label
  telling everyone about
  their achievements.
* Use Circle Time as a
  time for children to
  show what they can do.

38

Individual needs

✧ Toddler or baby toys with switches and buttons are good for children with additional needs.

✧ Find toys that make a noise to attract the attention of those who need it.

✧ Take digital photos of what they can do to show to children themselves. Make individual 'I Can' photo books.

Safety Tip!

✻ Make sure all electrical equipment is safe and regularly checked. Always stay near children who are working with electrical equipment.

Watch, listen, reflect

👁 Note how children listen and follow your instructions.

👁 Listen to them using new words and sounds.

👁 Look to see if the children have the confidence to try new activities and take turns to operate the toys. Can they wait, take a turn, perform a song, work together?

Working together

Parents could:

* Help their children to learn how to use simple, safe equipment at home.
* Reward their children's successes and achievement with smiles, hugs and words, not just with material rewards.

Practitioners could:

* Put up notices and photos about children's achievements in learning.
* Encourage parents to teach their children to be independent as soon as they can manage it.

I Can Do It

Confidence and competence

What are they learning?

are they
  having fun?
  learning new skills?
  concentrating?
  succeeding?
this leads to
  * self esteem
  * sustained attention
  * turn taking

Confidence and competence

Walkers, talkers and pretenders

Aspect:
A Strong Child
Components:
developing self assurance

Circle Time - recognising success

What you need

* big sheets of pale green and brown paper
* scissors
* felt pens

What you do

This activity can start with the whole group, and then become an ongoing source of interest in the setting.

1. Before you start, cut out a trunk and branches of a tree from brown paper. Make it big enough to fit on a display board or screen. Work with some children to cut out some leaves, about 20cm (4.5") long from green paper.
2. Gather the children together and talk to them about the 'Can Do' tree. Pin the tree trunk up on the wall where they can see it.
3. Now explain that the leaves on the tree are very special, because each one is about what they can do.
4. Talk to them about the things they can do. Write each name and something he or she can do on a leaf and pin them on the branches of the tree.

Ready for more?

* Add photos of the children, showing what they can do.
* Children and adults could draw pictures of the things they can do and add them to the tree.

Individual needs

- Small steps and tiny achievements need recognising for children with learning or developmental difficulties. Make sure you celebrate these small steps.
- Invite parents into your setting regularly to share your pleasure in their child's achievements.

Tiny Tip

✻ make sure every child is represented on the tree and that personal skills and attributes are celebrated too.

Watch, listen, reflect

- Listen to what children say about their own achievements and what they feel they can do.
- Watch as you work with children and remember the new learning or significant achievements in their social or emotional development. use these to make new leaves for the 'Can Do' tree.

Working together

Parents could:

* Tell practitioners about the new things their child can do at home.
* Come into your setting and look at the achievements of their chid and others in the group.

Practitioners could:

* Ask parents to add leaves to the tree when their child learns something new..
* Make sure the 'Can Do' tree is up to date - by sending home the old leaves as new things are learned or demonstrated.

I Can Do It

Confidence and competence

What are they learning?

are they
involved?
talking about what they can do?
having fun?
recognising achievements?

this leads to
* confidence
* self esteem and awareness

I Can Do It

Confidence and competence

Walkers, talkers and pretenders

Aspect:
A Strong Child
Components:
developing self assurance

What can you do with it? – an ideas game with photos

What you need
* some photos of equipment and activities in your setting (or you could use pictures from magazines, junk mail or catalogues)

What you do
This activity is suitable for up to four children.
1. Collect your pictures, select four, and put them <u>FACE UP</u> on a table or the carpet.
2. Give the children time to look at all the pictures and talk about who is in them and what is happening.
3. Now hold up each picture in turn and ask them 'What can you do with this game/toy?'
4. Let the children suggest what could be done. Accept and praise all realistic ideas.
5. Now put the photos down again and ask 'Which toy can you (*throw/ride on/build with/make a picture with*)?
6. Play the game again with new pictures or more pictures.

another idea:
* Sort the photos into equipment for riding, building, making.

Ready for more?
- Choose a piece of apparatus to talk about at group time. Discuss what you can do with it.
- Take photos of children using equipment in unusual or new ways. Put them on a display near that piece of equipment.

Individual needs

☼ Encourage children to experiment in different ways with equipment. Praise them when they come up with a new idea rather than copying what others do.

☼ Use the equipment rather than photos to make this activity easier to understand. Ask the child to show you what they can do.

Tiny Tip

❊ Display photos of children using the equipment in your setting, or make an ideas album of new uses of equipment.

Watch, listen, reflect

👁 Watch for children using equipment in new and imaginative ways.

👁 Listen for descriptive words and real thinking as children describe the uses of equipment.

👁 Watch to see if children to each other and use the new ideas after the discussion activity.

👁 Note new ideas and vocabulary used during discussion.

Working together

Parents could:

* Encourage their children to talk about the things they make and do.
* Tell practitioners about the new ways their children have used toys and games.

Practitioners could:

* Encourage children to select and put away activities and resources. Make sure equipment is accessible, and encourage children to use all resources flexibly. Sometimes children surprise us with their ingenuity of we let them!

I Can Do It

Confidence and competence

What are they learning?

are they
  thinking?
  remembering?
  listening?
  learning new
  ideas?
this leads to
  * independence
  * confidence
  * innovation

43

Confidence and competence

Aspect:
A Strong Child
Components:
developing self assurance

Resources

Bakets and other containers, weaving materials, dolly pegs,
Mindstretchers
Tel: 07768 882537

Scissors, including those for left handers and children with poor grip
ASCO Suppliers
Tel: 0113 2707070

A good value, easy to use desktop digital printer:
Hewlett Packard
HP Photosmart 230

Tents and Tunnels
Get pop up tents from seaside shops.

Posting boxes, stacking rings, bean bags, threading toys and peg boards, rolling toys, simple instruments and musical rollers from:
ASCO Suppliers
Tel: 0113 2707070

Heuristic Play
Find out more about heuristic play in 'People Under Three' by Elinor Goldschmied and Sonia Jackson

Books
The Little Book of Treasure Baskets
The Little Book of Nursery Rhymes
The Little Book of Circle Time

all available from Featherstone Education

Songs and rhymes

These songs and rhymes are all suitable for developing hands, fingers, feet and fine motor skills. They are all in This Little Puffin (Penguin Books) or in The Little Book of Nursery Rhymes (Featherstone Education).

Songs for babies

Rock a bye baby
Ride a Cock Horse
Row, row, row the boat
Dance to your Daddy
Bye Baby Bunting
Hush Little Baby Don't you Cry
Down among the fishes in the deep
  blue sea

This Little Puffin has a whole
  section of baby songs

Some Finger songs & rhymes

This Little Pig Went to Market
Pat-a-cake, pat-a-cake
Round and round the garden
She didn't dance
Incy Wincy Spider
Tommy Thumb
Five Little Peas
Two Little Dicky Birds
Wind the Bobbin
My Little House
Here are the Lady's Knives & Forks
Here is a Box
One Potato, Two Potato
Peter Hammers with one hammer
One finger, One Thumb Keep Moving
Heads, Shoulders, Knees and Toes
Roly, Poly up and Down
Teddy Bear, Teddy Bear

Aspect:
A Strong Child
Components:
developing self assurance

45

The Little Baby Book Series

The structure of the series has been developed to support the Birth to Three Matters Guidance, issued in 2003 by the DfES/Sure Start. The series is structured to follow the aspects contained within the guidance:

Purple Books support the development of a Strong Child:
> a child who is secure, confident and aware of him\herself, feeling a valued and important member of their family, their group and their setting.

Pink Books support the development of a Skilful Communicator:
> a child who is sociable, good at communicating with adults and other children, listens and communicates with confidence, who enjoys and plays with words in discussion, stories, songs and rhymes.

Green Books support the development of a Competent Learner:
> a child who uses play to explore and make sense of their world, creating, imagining, and representing their experiences.

Blue Books support the development of a Healthy Child:
> a child who is well nourished and well supported, feels safe and protected, and uses that sense of security to grow, both physically and emotionally, becoming independent and able to make choices in their play and learning.

The First Four books (Published in April 2003) are:
> **What I Really Want** (Purple Books)
> **I Like You, You Like Me** (Pink Books)
> **Touch it Feel it** (Green Books)
> **Grab and let Go** (Blue Books)

The next four books (also containing one book from each aspect) are published in October 2003.